A BRIEF WORD FROM THE AUTHOR

There are quite a number of snakes being sold in the pet hobby these days...as I slowly move down the crowded aisles of so many herpetocultural swap meets and breeder expos, I see them—the Gray-banded Kingsnakes, the albino Corn Snakes (of one variety or another, or another, or another...), the Emerald Tree Boas (it has always been a mystery to me as to why these nasty creatures are so popular), plus I also see some other herptiles beyond the serpents—poison frogs, tortoises, Green Iguanas (by the ton), albino horned frogs (more like lethargic lumps of pork fat), and so on.

But then, every now and again, someone with remarkably good taste has a Pine Snake, or one of its relatives, for sale. I have seen many of the species and subspecies, and in a number of color varieties too. Many of these snakes were virtually unknown until the hobbyists got their hands on a few, and I support such things. For example, who ever even knew about the Black Pine Snake or the Louisiana Pine Snake twenty years ago? There was the literature, of course (thanks to wonderful people like Olive Griffith Stull), but the specimens were as rare as lunar eclipses. Now, the Black Pine is fairly common, and the Louisiana Pine is catching up (this one is still quite expensive, but fascinating nevertheless). A handful of the Mexican *Pituophis* are also being captive-bred (I had the honor of seeing a neonatal *Pituophis deppei* in Orlando, Florida last year that made my mouth water), and there are even a number of albino, striped, and patternless *Pituophis* varieties one could choose from (the albino Florida

Breeding captive snakes has become something of an art form over the last decade. Now, species that were once considered rare, like this Black Pine Snake, *Pituophis melanoleucus lodingi*, can be purchased and kept by any interested hobbyist.

W. P. MARA

W. P. MARA

The Louisiana Pine Snake, *Pituophis melanoleucus ruthveni*, still has never been seen by most hobbyists. There are, however, a few breeders trying to correct this problem by producing handsome captive-bred specimens like the one shown here.

Pines, incidentally, are among the most gorgeous products of captive-breeding ever created. That one snake alone could turn captive-breeding from a hobby into an art form).

Anyone who is interested in snakes and doesn't look into the Pine Snakes and their kin is simply missing out on a great thing. The snakes of the genus *Pituophis* are just...amazing. They are gorgeous, hardy, they eat like pigs (...no, change that—pigs eat like the snakes of the genus *Pituophis*, or at least *wish* they could), and they are easy to breed in captivity. Most species that are currently commercially available aren't even *expensive*! Like I said—amazing.

I wrote this book for the serious enthusiast. In it, you'll find a lot of information that will help you keep and breed a Pine Snake or one of its many relatives, and for as long a time as you wish. Longevity of the specimens is, after all, the keeper's ultimate goal; and I hope you achieve it.

Good luck.

W. P. Mara
May, 1994

DEDICATION
To He who has taken my hand and led me down this long and winding road. As one day finally draws to a slow a gentle close, the warmth of another begins to make itself known to me...

THE GENUS *PITUOPHIS*

The snakes of the genus *Pituophis*, known in vernacular terms as the Pine Snakes, Bullsnakes, and the Gopher Snakes (but referred to in the remainder of this book as the Pine Snakes and kin, the Pine Snakes and their relatives, or simply the Pine Snakes), are among the most beautiful of all North American serpents. There are currently five accepted species with a multitude of subspecies, all of which will be mentioned in this chapter to some degree. I would like to point out that there has been a great amount of conflict concerning the exact taxonomy of the genus, particularly in regard to the number of species and/or subspecies (the main gripe being which ones should be recognized as full species and which should remain simple subspecies), but, all in all, the statements I will make in regards to the systematic arrangement will be mine and mine alone. I will cover each known

This is a rocky, wooded hillside in north-central Baja California, home of the Central Baja California Gopher Snake, *Pituophis catenifer bimaris*. Quiet locales such as this are the home of many members of the genus *Pituophis*.

variation of *Pituophis*, but where they are placed categorically will be of my own choosing (although I will, of course, stick to what I feel have been the most common and rational routes). I apologize in advance to anyone who takes offense to my perspectives, as there doubtlessly are those who easily can become aroused by such things.

GENERAL RANGE

The genus *Pituophis* is native mainly to the North American continent, from as far north as southern Canada, then south into Central America in Guatemala; the majority of the species occur in the United States. They can be found on both U. S. coasts, plus there are a few subspecies on satellite islands off the western coast of Baja California.

HABITAT

Pine Snakes and their relatives, although geographically widespread, are found in only a few different habitats. Pine forests are a very common locale, as are grassy, treeless prairies. They have been found in both lowlands and high on mountains, plus in quiet wooded areas (reasonably far from water, relative to most other snakes), desert regions, and on farms. They seem to prefer sandy, loamy soils whenever possible, and spend much of their time in and around animal burrows.

BEHAVIOR AND HABITS

Pine Snakes and their kin have a reputation for being somewhat temperamental, and in truth I can't really say I would argue with this. However, it should be pointed out that while many snakes of the genus *Pituophis* are likely to put on a very fierce display of bad temper, most of them are not apt to bite. This is not to say they will *never* bite (and it

should be kept in mind that the bite of a large Pine Snake can be considerable), but for the most part, these snakes only put on a good display—rearing back, vibrating their tails (which, when done under a pile of loose leaf litter, produces a very intimidating effect), and hissing in such a loud fashion that it almost sounds like air escaping from a punctured car tire. During this hissing, the Pine Snakes will open their jaws slightly and even allow their forked tongues to dangle limply, which, in combination with the "mean" look of their dark eyes, can riddle the heart of a causal observer with a great amount of fear. In short, they are very impressive bluffers (I state for the record that I have handled hundreds of *Pituophis* and have only been bitten once).

THE SPECIES AND THE SUBSPECIES

As mentioned earlier, there are five species in the genus *Pituophis*, most with their own group of subspecies (only one species—*Pituophis sayi* (the Bullsnake)—is monotypic). Each will be discussed in reasonable detail here.

Pituophis catenifer—Gopher Snake

Growing to length of about 110 in/ 275 cm, the Gopher Snake is one of the most handsome snakes in North America. The base color varies with the subspecies, but the basic ground colors are yellow, tan, or cream, with a series of medium-sized dorsal blotches of either black, brown, or reddish. Some specimens have tiny reddish or orange spots and speckles between the blotches, and these snakes are remarkably attractive. Along the laterum there are even more blotches, these being considerably smaller than those on the dorsum; the overall pattern, in fact, is not unlike that of many

K. H. SWITAK

The San Diego Gopher Snake, *Pituophis catenifer annectans*, can be distinguished by its 65 to 106 body blotches (which are usually rounded and dark brown or black in color) and its attractive ground color of brownish tan or wheat-yellow.

W. P. MARA

One of the more popular, and certainly more visually striking, members of the *Pituophis* group, the Cape Gopher Snake, *Pituophis catenifer vertebralis*, is native only to the extreme southern area of Baja California. It has between 38 and 51 body blotches which, as you can see here, start off ruby-reddish at the head, then become black as they approach the tail.

rattlesnake species, and thus many Gopher Snakes are mistaken for rattlers and killed on sight. There is almost always a dark line running from the corner of the jaw, through the eye, across the top of the head, then through the opposite eye and down to the jaw corner again. The belly is usually a white, off-white, or very light pale yellow, sometimes with a peppering of dark spots. Some specimens, usually those found in California, can have stripes rather than blotches, and many of these are currently being bred and sold in the herpetocultural hobby. They are reasonably priced and very, very attractive. A few are even patternless, but these are, of course, selectively bred and can be rather expensive.

The range of the Gopher Snake can be described in general terms as covering most of the western quarter of the United States, just reaching into Canada, and south all through Baja California and part of Mexico.

Gopher Snakes are generally diurnal, have a propensity for climbing (more so than most other *Pituophis*), and feed mostly on rodents and small birds. Some specimens have been known to accept a variety of small reptiles, and a few young Gopher Snakes have been known to attack large insects, but these cases are the exception rather than the rule. Gopher Snakes breed from April to May and lay eggs in early summer. Clutches range from only a few to two dozen. The young measure about a foot in length.

Facing Page: The Bullsnake, *Pituophis sayi*, shown in its native habitat. Bullsnakes are diurnal ground-dwellers that move through grassy prairies and rocky woodlands in search of any small mammals they can find. They are efficient hunters with very powerful constrictive abilities. Photo by K. H. Switak.

The Great Basin Gopher Snake, *Pituophis catenifer deserticola*, is one of the Gopher Snakes not often seen in captivity. It has a fairly wide range, stretching over much of the western third of the United States, and was first described by Dr. Leonhard Stejneger in 1893. Photo by R. D. Bartlett.

Subspecies—
P. c. affinis (Sonoran Gopher Snake)
P. c. annectans (San Diego Gopher
   Snake)
P. c. bimaris (Baja California Gopher
   Snake)
P. c. catenifer (Pacific Gopher
   Snake)
P. c. coronalis (Coronado Gopher
   Snake)
P. c. deserticola (Great Basin Gopher
   Snake)
P. c. fulginatus (San Martin Gopher
   Snake)
P. c. insulanus (Cedros Island Gopher
   Snake)

P. c. pumilis (Santa Cruz Gopher
   Snake)
P. c. vertebralis (Cape Gopher Snake)

Pituophis melanoleucus–Pine Snake
   Perhaps the most visually striking
species of the whole genus, the Pine
Snake grows to a length of about 66
in/168 cm and can be seen in a
variety of colors and patterns,
depending on which of the four
subspecies you're dealing with. With
the nominate form, the Northern Pine
Snake, *P. m. melanoleucus*, you have
a snake that is basically white, with
very dark dorsal blotches. Further
black spotting and speckling occurs
on the laterum and the dorsolaterum.
The belly is usually a brilliant white
with little or no markings at all. The
keeled scales are very sharp, giving
the animal a very "rough" feel. It is
heavy bodied and looks quite
powerful, which it is. Then there is
the Florida Pine Snake, *P. m.
mugitus*, which looks like a vague
Northern Pine, the blotches being
lighter brown or, in very pretty
specimens, almost a light brownish
lavender (and usually referred to by
herpetoculturists as the "Lavender
Phase" variety). The arrangement of
the Florida Pine Snake's pattern and
color is, in fact, so variable that some
specimens could be considered
absolutely gorgeous whereas others
are utterly sodden with ugliness.
After the Florida Pine you have the
rare Louisiana Pine Snake, *P. m.
ruthveni*, which looks, in short, like
an ugly Northern Pine in the sense
that the dark colors are "messier,"
i.e., less well-defined. This snake is
considered by some taxonomists to
be a full species, which of course has
no bearing on its appearance, but
suggests that although it looks a lot
like the Northern Pine, it may no
longer be related to it on the
subspecific level due to its geographic

independence. Finally, there is the Black Pine Snake, *P. m. lodingi*, which, as you can guess by its common name, is more or less a totally black snake; however, this is only the case in full-grown adults. When Black Pines emerge from the egg, they resemble the Northern Pine so much that a casual observer probably couldn't delineate them. The darkness creeps in with age, consuming almost the entire snake (the dorsolateral region near and on the tail usually shows vague traces of pattern). This snake could simply be a melanistic population one of the other Pines (probably *P. m. melanoleucus*), but at the moment this is only a theory. The bottom line is, an adult Black Pine in good shape is an absolutely stunning animal, strongly reminiscent of the Eastern Indigo Snake, *Drymarchon corais couperi*, except that the Black Pine lacks the purplish/orange chin and is easier to acquire commercially.

The range of the Pine Snakes is, very generally, the southeastern quarter of the United States. I say generally because although this is the only area where the species occurs (the only other population is that of the Northern Pine Snake in southern New Jersey), the populations are scattered and fractured in many places. The Northern Pine, for example, also occurs in the Carolinas, Georgia, plus a few other states, and also overlaps with the Florida Pine in the northern part of the latter's range. The Black Pine can only be found along the Gulf Coast, as can the

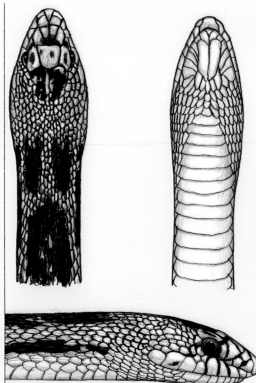

The head of the Northern Pine Snake, *Pituophis melanoleucus melanoleucus*. Notice the dark lines separating the upper lip scales (also known as the supralabials), and the enlarged snout (rostral scale). Illustration by John R. Quinn.

Louisiana Pine, which is remarkably scarce to begin with (it only occurs in western Louisiana and a small part of extreme eastern Texas).

Pine Snakes are active mainly during the day, although many will turn crepuscular and even nocturnal during intolerably hot weather. They spend most of their time on the ground, but have been known to climb through shrubs and trees in search of food. Their main diet is small mammals, i.e., mice, rats, voles, gophers, squirrels, rabbits, etc., but they also seem to have a liking for birds and their eggs. They are not known to be cannibalistic or show a taste for any other reptiles or amphibians. They are veteran burrowers, which is morphologically

evident by their pointed snout boasting the enlarged rostral scale. They are quite temperamental when disturbed, hissing and vibrating their tails with great speed. Be careful—some specimens will bite.

Subspecies—
P. m. lodingi (Black Pine Snake)
P. m. melanoleucus (Northern Pine Snake)
P. m. mugitus (Florida Pine Snake)
P. m. ruthveni (Louisiana Pine Snake)

*Pituophis sayi–***Bullsnake**
One of the largest of all North American serpents, this beast can grow up to a length of over 80 in/203 cm (the record being 100 in/254 cm). The general ground color of the Bullsnake is yellow, with a series of beautiful and clearly defined dark dorsal blotches being either black, dark brown, or light brown, usually outlined with darker stenciling. These blotches are clearest towards both the head and tail, those in the mid-region being slightly weaker. There are more blotches on the laterum, these also being a darker color than the dorsum. The dorsal blotches usually number somewhere around 45. The belly is a light yellowish color with strong dark markings, mostly near the sides. The head has a dark stripe running from the angle of the jaw to the eye, and usually there is a light yellow band running above it. The scales are very

Facing Page: The San Diego Gopher Snake, *Pituophis catenifer annectans*, was first described by Baird and Girard in 1853. The type-locality was recorded simply as "San Diego, California," and the original specimen, a subadult male, was collected sometime between May and September of 1850 by John L. LeConte, whose surname was utilized in conjunction with the classification of the Longnose Snake, *Rhinocheilus lecontei*. Photo by Peggy A. Vargas.

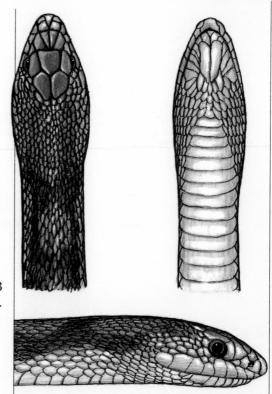

The head of the Cape Gopher Snake, *Pituophis catenifer vertebralis*. Notice the lack of dark markings; this is a fairly reliable characteristic of the subspecies. Illustration by John R. Quinn.

heavily keeled.
You can find the Bullsnake over a very large area. Its general range can be described as "most of the middle of the United States," but it also ranges north into Canada (southern Alberta), and south into northeastern Mexico. In the more southwestern part of its range, it overlaps with the Sonoran Gopher Snake, *Pituophis catenifer affinis*.

The Bullsnake is a creature of varied habitats, but the most common seem to be rolling plains and prairies; any quiet, open area, in fact. The Bullsnake is a fairly retiring creature, moving through low

ROBERT T. ZAPPALORTI

The Florida Pine Snake, *Pituophis melanoleucus mugitus*, is a strange creature in the sense that it can be seen in two abstract color/pattern varieties—beautiful, or ugly; the specimen shown seems to belong to the former. The Florida Pine can be found mostly in Florida, but also occurs in Georgia, Alabama, and South Carolina.

vegetation, grassy patches, and lurking through mammal burrows during the day (or, in the more southerly parts of its rage, at night when the weather gets too hot). It is quite fond of mice, rats, and other such furry creatures, but also has a marked propensity for feeding on birds and their eggs. It is a bold snake, rearing back when angered and hissing very loudly. Furthermore, most snakes of this species are not afraid to strike, and their bites can be remarkably painful. A large Bullsnake is a creature that

Facing Page: Follow these few morphological characteristics to identify the Central Baja California Gopher Snake, *Pituophis catenifer bimaris*—an instinct postorbital or prefrontal stripe, body blotches that are black near the head and on the tail but lightening to brown at midbody, and a ground color of yellow or orangish. Photo by K. H. Switak.

should be given considerable respect.

Subspecies—
   None

Pituophis deppei and *Pituophis lineaticollis*—The Mexican Pine Snakes

A collective discussion will be given for these two species because there is not a lot of information available about them to begin with. Only *P. deppei* is ever seen in the herpetocultural hobby, and then only at fairly high prices (although it should be pointed out, with some pride, that there is a select group of breeders turning out some remarkably beautiful specimens of this most striking animal).

Undoubtedly the least-studied species of the genus *Pituophis*, the two Mexican forms are also, sadly

Right: The Black Pine Snake, *Pituophis melanoleucus lodingi*.

Facing Page: The Bullsnake, *Pituophis sayi*, is the widest-ranging of all *Pituophis* species, covering the majority of the middle United States, then north into Canada and south into Mexico. It is a handsome and powerfully built snake, some specimens reaching up to 72 in/ 183 cm in length. Photo by John Iverson.

Below: Closeup of the scales of a Northern Pine Snake, *Pituophis melanoleucus melanoleucus* (a very red specimen—some examples of this snake will go through a red phase, although most of the time it will not be as pronounced as that on the snake shown here). Notice the heavy keeling and the apical pitting. This is a trademark of the genus. Photo by W. P. Mara.

K. H. SWITAK

There is a sort-of "micro-group" of *Pituophis* in Mexico that consists of two species—*P. deppei* and *P. lineaticollis*—each with two subspecies apiece. The snake shown here is *P. d. jani* (no known common name), which was first discovered in Buena Vista (probably in Coahuila), and described by Olive Griffith Stull in 1932.

enough, among the prettiest. There are four varieties altogether, each species having two subspecies apiece. With *P. d. deppei*, you have a basically tan-colored snake with very dark, fairly well-defined blotches ranging in color from dark brown to black. There is also some dark spotting on the laterum as well, but not much. The head is slightly lighter in color than the dorsum, and the chin is a buff color. The belly can also be buff, sometimes tending more toward an immaculate white. The

other subspecies, *P. d. jani*, closely resembles *P. d. deppei* in most respects, but the blotches closer to the head tend to be quite dark whereas those toward the rear will be lighter; with the nominate subspecies the color of the blotches remains more consistent.

With the nominate form of the other species, *P. l. lineaticollis*, you have a brownish base color and a pair of dark stripes that run from the back of the head to about one-third the snake's body length. The head is very plainly colored, and just slightly lighter than the rest of the body, although not much. With the second subspecies, *P. l. gibsoni*, you have a snake that looks very much like the nominate form, except that the striping can be more fractured rather than in one continual strip, and beyond that striping there are blotches with lightly colored centers.

The Mexican *Pituophis* are usually active during the day, hunting for birds and small mammals, and, like their cousins in the United States, are very bold and will gladly make a great fuss when irritated. *P. deppei jani*, for example, is supposedly a very formidable animal, particularly wild adults; they are among the few *Pituophis* that will not hesitate to bite.

In captivity, however, both Mexican species do very well and reportedly can be persuaded to reproduce without too much trouble on the keeper's part. Three of the four forms are native to, but not exclusive to, the Mexican Plateau. *P. l. gibsoni*, on the other hand, can be found as far south as the highlands of Guatemala, making it the most southerly ranging snake of this genus.

Subspecies—
P. d. deppei (no known common name)
P. d. jani (no known common name)
P. l. lineaticollis (no known common name)
P. l. gibsoni (no known common name.

Interestingly, one of the central characteristics of the Mexican *Pituophis* is the fact that they have only two prefrontal scales rather than the four found on all other forms of *Pituophis*. The two scales in question can be clearly seen on this *Pituophis deppei*.

R. D. BARTLETT

HOUSING

The housing of the Pine Snakes and their kin is a fairly straightforward deal, keeping mind of course that some specimens will grow to about 6 ft/180 cm, which, I suppose, is not terribly alarming if you consider the fact that a Reticulated Python, *Python reticulatus*, can grow up to 28 ft/840 cm! Although the snakes of the genus *Pituophis* may be among the largest serpents in all of North America, they are still quite small compared to our friend the "Retic," plus so many other snakes worldwide, and that, of course, is comforting news for all herpeto-culturists who don't fancy the idea of keeping really large snakes.

Climatic requirements are also undemanding with the Pine Snake contingent, as are cage furnishing requirements and so on. In fact, I would be willing to go so far as to say

Facing Page: The Northern Pine Snake, *Pituophis melanoleucus melanoleucus*, is one of the most popular *Pituophis* in the herpetocultural hobby. It is found primarily in scattered locations in the southeastern United States, but there is also a large population in southern New Jersey. Photo by Robert T. Zappalorti.

the snakes of this group are among the easiest to house and maintain, mainly because they are so very hardy. As long as you can provide a comfortable amount of space for them, you'll have no problems whatsoever.

SIZE OF THE ENCLOSURE

So, how big of an enclosure will you need? That, of course, depends on the size of your snake and how many you are keeping. A 20-gallon "long" glass aquarium seems appropriate for either a few neonates, two subadults, or one adult (although I would personally go up to a 30-gallon for a full-sized adult *Pituophis*). Beyond that, a 55-gallon will comfortably house an adult breeding pair or four subadults (or a whole mess of neonates). From the examples given, you can pretty much ascertain what size tank you will need for the snakes you've got. I won't give recommendations for mundane curiosities like, "What size tank will you need to keep eight full-sized adults?" since, obviously, only a masochist would keep this many large snakes in the same enclosure in

PHOTO COURTESY OF HAGEN

Pine Snakes and their kin can range in size from about one foot to over five feet, so it is important that you obtain an enclosure of appropriate size for the specimen(s) you have. Check your local pet shop for the tank you'll need.

the first place (answer: build four large cement walls in your backyard and start your own snake pit).

ENCLOSURE COMPONENTS

Substrate

Now here's an issue that has garnered its own collection of differing opinions—what's the best type of cage bedding to use with Pine Snakes and their kin (or, for that matter, with most any reptile)?

The answer depends, to some degree, on your own needs and goals. If, for example, you want to submit yourself to the rigors of maintaining a very naturalistic "show tank," then something like newspapers probably won't do. Conversely, if you want to stick with simplicity and ease of cleaning, then something heavy to work with like gravel will be inadequate. If we look at a few of the more reliable substrates, at least you'll have enough information to make your own decision.

Gravel: The classic standby, so popular with those who keep freshwater fishes. Gravel can be bought in an array of attractive colors at just about any pet shop on earth. Gravel is reasonably priced and can be used time and time again. Furthermore, it is safe to use with Pine Snakes and their relatives. Problems? Gravel is reproachfully heavy and may give you a hernia when you try to lug buckets of it around during cleaning time.

Potting Soil: The most basic and easy to acquire of all substrates is ordinary potting soil, which can be bought in bags at any garden store. Potting soil is most often used in terrariums for frogs, salamanders, and so on, and has the advantage of being able to support plant life. This, of course, may not be of great appeal to the keeper of Pine Snakes and their kin, but you never know. Potting soil also creates a very realistic setting and can be maintained with ease. A fair word of warning, however—don't use the potting soil you find in your own backyard, because you never know what might be crawling around in it.

Wood Shavings: Always a popular cage medium in the herpetocultural field, wood shavings can be

PHOTO COURTESY OF HAGEN

Wood shavings often are utilized in conjunction with snakes. As long as you purchase those of the pine variety, you should have no problems. Wood shavings are inexpensive, absorbent, and easy to work with.

bought at most any pet store that stocks small mammals, it is fairly cheap, can be disposed of, and is easy to work with because it's so light. On the downside, there have been reports of sharp pieces of wood shavings being swallowed by captive snakes, then poking holes in their intestinal walls. Not good. Also (not that this matters to many keepers), pine shavings are not very attractive. One final comment—if you do decide to use wood shavings, avoid those of the cedar variety because the oils are toxic to snakes. Those of the pine variety are acceptable (and less expensive anyway).

Sand: Not a bad choice, especially if you're going for that desert look (which we'll discuss shortly). Sand is

If you want to add a little life to an otherwise dull tank setup, you should purchase a piece of scenic sheeting. Available at many pet shops, these sheets can be placed right onto the outside back wall of a glass tank and are offered in a variety of tableaux.

inexpensive, attractive, and does wonders for drying up feces, which makes cleaning fairly easy (most of the time you just scoop it up). The only real complaints I've ever heard about sand are the fact that it can be very heavy, which, again, might make it tough to deal with during cleaning, and some keepers claim that snakes occasionally develop skin irritations from extended contact with sand. I suppose this might be true in the case of snakes that really don't slide across that much sand in the wild, but I have to confess that I have never had this problem with any of my own snakes.

Indoor/Outdoor Carpeting or "Artificial Turf": Now, this stuff isn't particularly bad. It comes in a variety of colors (the two main ones being brown and green), it is fairly inexpensive, can be used repeatedly, and is available at your local pet store in pre-cut sizes to fit tanks. Perfect, huh? Pretty much. A few

problems to keep in mind—Pine Snakes and the rest of their gang tend to be a little filthy, so you may find yourself taking everything out of their enclosure and then washing the carpeting on a fairly regular basis. Also, scrubbing the carpeting too hard sometimes causes the fibers to fall off, but if you don't scrub them hard enough they won't get clean. Aside from these two little points, indoor/outdoor carpeting, or "artificial turf" (or whatever else it's being called this week), really isn't all that bad. And it looks pretty good, too.

Newspaper: For anyone who keeps lots and lots of snakes, this is a pretty reasonable substrate. Think about it—newspaper certainly is cheap, it is light and easy to work with, fairly absorbent (you'd think it was designed just for the purpose of having snakes defecate on it, but then a lot of them don't really have a great amount of value beyond that to begin with), and there certainly is an endless supply of it. Of course, the most obvious downside to newspaper is that (snakes can't read) it is not terribly pleasing to the eye (maybe the Sunday comics perhaps), but when you've got thirty or forty tanks to worry about, visual benevolence is the last thing on your mind. Some keepers have expressed concern over the ink on newspaper and what effect it has on the snakes. Since I am not of the type who has used newspaper extensively for this purpose, I cannot really say I have ever witnessed any negative effects firsthand, but the assumption that something might go amiss certainly isn't without reason.

Paper Towels: The last and, in my humble opinion, the best substrate to use with any snakes. Paper towels are inexpensive, very absorbent, super-easy to work with, and, as far as I'm concerned, don't really look all that bad. Since one of the central goals of snake-keeping is to keep your animals alive for as long as you possibly can, something like paper toweling is ideal because it is so inert. If you have a lot of snake tanks and don't really place a great price on visuality, I would say soft, uncolored paper towels are the ideal substrate for you.

Rocks

All snake tanks should have some rocks in them, and at least one should be fairly good-sized. Why? Because, if nothing else, rocks provide a snake with a good place to begin a shed on. Without a surface as abrasive as a rock, a snake's shed might adhere to the animal's face and that can cause real problems. Beyond this most rudimentary reason, rocks are an attractive addition to any natural tank. They can be purchased at most any pet store or landscaper's

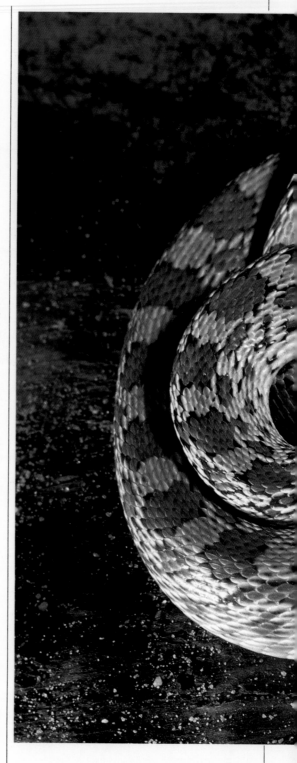

Although the snakes of the genus *Pituophis* are among the largest serpents in North America, none of them normally grow over a length of about 72 in/183 cm, so the provision of adequate housing should not be a problem. The snake shown is a young Bullsnake, *Pituophis sayi*. Photo by B. Kahl.

supply house, are inexpensive, and are available, obviously, in many different shapes and sizes. If you have the ambition and skill, you can build little rock caves for your pets. This can be done either by simply piling the rocks together ever-so-carefully (so the caves don't tumble down and hurt the snakes), or by cementing the rocks together. Finally, small Pine Snakes may use rocks to hide under or behind.

Waterbowls

A very important component in the enclosure of a *Pituophis*, waterbowls need to be one thing most of all—untippable. Since Pine Snakes and their relatives are so large, they will tip over normal bowls in no time at

Plants add a nice visual touch to any setup, and those that are artificial probably are better to use with snakes of the genus *Pituophis* because real plants will just get crushed over the course of time.

PHOTO COURTESY OF HAGEN

all, which means you get to have the fun of cleaning up the spill each time. The best kinds of waterbowls to use are either the plastic types that have wider bases than the mouths, or the really heavy ceramic ones, either of which can be found in pet stores. It should also be pointed out that waterbowls should never be filled more than halfway, and the water should be changed in a snake's bowl at least every other day. Pine Snakes need regular access to water and will drink often.

Plants (Real and Artificial)

Pine Snakes and their kin aren't really in dire need of any kind of plant life in their tank setups, but such items will add a nice touch of color and naturalness. With large Pine Snakes, live plants may get plowed over as the snakes go about their daily business, but this is a risk you'll have to take. False plants are more sensible than live ones because at least these only have to be set back up again; live plants may get destroyed completely, and what's the point of that? Artificial plants can be obtained at most any pet store and are offered in a variety of sizes and colors.

Hideboxes

Snakes of the genus *Pituophis* are fairly active creatures that do most of their business during the day. However, when they retreat to their places of rest, those places are usually underground, i.e., mammal burrows and so forth, Therefore, it is advised that you provide them with a hidebox that somehow replicates this sensation of "going down." This can be done fairly easily by including a hidebox that has its entrance hole cut not through the side, but the top. The box itself can be made of many things, but the most popular are

W. P. MARA

Hideboxes can be made from just about anything. The keys to remember with hideboxes are sturdiness, security (for the snake), and cleanability. The snake shown is a juvenile Northern Pine Snake, *Pituophis melanoleucus melanoleucus*.

wood or cork (in natural setups), or plastic shoe or sweaterboxes (in clinical setups). The whole purpose of a hidebox is to provide a snake with a place of privacy, so remember to keep the box covered well. On the other hand, the hidebox should also be fully accessible to the keeper for purposes of cleaning and so on, so don't set up a hidebox in such a way that you'll never be able to get in to it!

Backdrops

For the sake of decoration, many keepers like to use scenic backdrops on their Pine Snake tanks. For those of you who aren't sure what these are, they are simply large color posters (sort of) that depict various natural scenery. Such backdrops can be purchased at virtually any pet store (there are all kinds, and not

only for reptiles and amphibians), they are reasonably priced, and they add a nice visual touch to most any setup. Although it would be foolish to say these backdrops actually help you with the keeping of the animal involved, they are, by the same token, completely harmless.

CLIMATE CONTROL

Heat

Since snakes of the genus *Pituophis* are cold-blooded and occur in a temperate region, they will need to be provided with some sort of heat source—an ambient temperature of about 82°F/28°C is what you're after (a slight reduction during the night hours is acceptable too). Fortunately, there are many ways in which a keeper can do this. Thanks to the immense popularity of snake-keeping, the pet market offers the interested keeper a wide variety of products.

One is the under-tank heating pad. In many ways, this is the most superior method of providing heat for snakes. Why? For one, only a single spot is heated, which affords the snake the freedom to move onto or away from this spot whenever it wants to. Furthermore, heating pads can be used without having to sacrifice tank security, i.e., running a wire into the tank and leaving a gap in the cover. One hint concerning heating pads—there are a few that are made to stick to the bottom of the tank, but the adherent substance is *so* adherent, you could probably slap the pad onto the Space Shuttle and it wouldn't come off during re-entry into the earth's atmosphere. This, of course, means you'll have problems if you want to use a certain pad on a different tank from the one it's already on. However, if you wrap the pad in tin foil, all you have to do is slip it under a tank and remove it whenever you wish.

Another method of heating is the spot lamp, which simply warms a certain area (i.e., a basking spot) in the tank via a heat lamp suspended overhead. Heat lamps can be purchased at many pet stores and are reasonably inexpensive. They are very sensible with snake-keeping and can be used with other herptiles as well. If you set up a timer in conjunction with a heat lamp so it turns off during the night hours, you will replicate the natural effect.

Finally, simple ambient heat, provided by a room heater, suits the needs of many keepers, particularly those that have many tanks (since buying a heating pad or heat lamp for every single tank is frightfully impractical). Heaters of the ceramic

A very sensible way to heat a snake's tank is through the use of an under-tank heating pad. These pads create warmth in one particular location, allowing a snake to either move onto or away from the spot whenever it wishes. Photo courtesy of Zoo Med Laboratories.

variety are the most sensible, being small, inexpensive, and cost-effective in regards to your electric bill. Set the heater up with a thermostat (if your heater doesn't already have a thermostat built in) and you're ready to roll. The only downside to providing heat this way is if the surrounding temperature gets *too* hot, a snake will not be able to move out of it (except, perhaps, into the waterbowl).

Light/Photoperiod

The word photoperiod essentially means the amount of daylight that an animal is exposed to. With Pine Snakes and their kin, the amount of daylight they should receive during the active season is around 12 to 15 hours per day, growing shorter as the autumn approaches.

The easiest way to make sure your snakes get the proper photoperiod is by hooking up your lighting

All the snakes of the genus *Pituophis* need heat to some degree. Those that live towards the southern end of the range, like this Mexican *Pituophis deppei jani*, will need a little more heat than those that occur in the North.

W. P. MARA

apparatus to a timer. This, of course, completely takes the responsibility off your shoulders. Timers can be purchased at most any department store, hardware store, or home-improvement center. Beyond using a timer, you can always park your snake's tank next to a window and let the sun do the job. Of course, there are drawbacks to this method, one being the question of what you should do if you have a lot of tanks. Also, windows can allow drafts, which spell trouble for captive snakes.

The quality of the light need not be anything beyond ordinary Tungsten. Many people who are familiar with keeping lizards or turtles will know what "full-spectrum" lighting is—light that replicates that given off by the sun. The nutrients therein are essential to the survival of lizards and turtles, particularly in the manufacturing of vitamin D3. With snakes, however, this need does not

exist, so you will not have to worry yourself with the expense that is usually incurred when purchasing a full-spectrum bulb. I would like to point out, however, that more than one professional breeder has made the claim that snakes exposed to full-spectrum light for about five or six hours per day give better breeding results. It seems the pairs are more willing to mate, the eggs are in better shape, and the clutch sizes seem a tiny bit larger. The truth, in any case, is that a little full-spectrum lighting won't hurt a Pine Snake either way, so it might be worth trying.

Moisture and Humidity

Since Pine Snakes and their kin occur in fairly dry regions, it is not generally necessary for a keeper to closely examine and worry over their moisture and humidity levels, except perhaps to assure that neither goes too high. With many amphibians, for

example, a daily misting of the inside walls of the enclosure is crucial to their survival; this is not the case with snakes of the genus *Pituophis*. In fact, you will want to make sure the tanks stay fairly dry, for too much moisture will give the snakes skin blisters and respiratory problems, which, of course, should be avoided. In short, the enclosure should be kept dry, not moist, and humidity should be fairly low. Pine Snakes and their relatives do not need added moisture.

SETTING UP THE TANK

There basically are three different tank setups you can arrange for your Pine Snakes—the Desert Setup, the Pine Woods Setup, and the Generic Equivalent Setup. Each of these requires a minimum of effort and can be easily maintained. The first two are "show tanks," and will boast a biotope of sorts, but, in reality, they are most valued for their visual appeal (a nicely arranged natural terrarium can be very, very impressive). The third, the Generic Equivalent, is keyed in to the concept of simplicity, sacrificing visual esthetics for ease of cleaning and clinical sensibility.

The Desert Setup

You start the Desert Setup by first washing the tank thoroughly (always start with a clean tank), and then filling it with about 2 in/5 cm of sand. Place in a few large rocks, arranging a few so the snakes have a place to hide (be very careful when doing this—you don't want your

Facing Page: Due to the fact that the Northern Pine Snake, *Pituophis melanoleucus melanoleucus*, occurs as far north in the United States as southern New Jersey, its heat requirements are not as severe as, say, the Baja California forms of *Pituophis*. Northern Pines can be kept at as low a temperature as 72°F/22°C during the summer months. Photo by R. D. Bartlett.

construction to come tumbling down on them), and then add in a waterbowl and any climate-control accessories. If you wish, you can find a few appropriate plants to give the setup some color; you can also litter the bedding with some smaller stones as well. Whenever a snake defecates, the soiled spot can be scooped up with a large spoon attached to the end of a stick. Not much more is required to arrange the Desert Setup, but then deserts don't have much to them anyway. The tank is simple, easy to clean, and inexpensive to create.

The Pine Woods Setup

In my opinion, a much more attractive arrangement than the Desert Setup. You begin with, again, a clean tank, then add in a two-inch layer of soft white sand (this may be hard to find, but in the New Jersey Pine Barrens, which I am familiar with, the sand is whitish gray and very loamy), then sprinkle on a layer of dried pine needles. After that, you will want to add in the rocks, and even a few large branches or, even better, a hollow log for the snake to hide in. Plants added into this setup look particularly nice, especially if you go to the trouble of finding species that are native to such an area. Add in the waterbowl and all climate-control items, and then you're finished.

The Generic Equivalent Setup

Finally, we come to the setup that focuses on simplicity—the Generic Equivalent. You begin with either a large glass aquarium or a large plastic tub. The substrate is paper towels or newspapers, with a hidebox furnished from something like a plastic shoebox with a hole cut into the lid. The waterbowl should also be plastic, and the only natural item included should be a rock so the snakes will have something to shed their skin on.

The beauty with this setup is, of course, the simplicity of maintenance; virtually anyone can manipulate something as light as a plastic tub. The other strong point is the fact that everything is so "safe," chances are a snake that is healthy will stay healthy. If, for example, you use soil as a substrate, as you would with a naturalistic design, there is always a chance that the soil could contain something like mite eggs. Or, if a snake defecates on a soil bedding, you may not even spot it for a day or two. Finally, the Generic Equivalent Setup is great for quarantining sick snakes; something you should keep in mind.

TANK CLEANING

This subheading really should be included in a chapter on diseases and so forth because cage cleaning is, without question, an affair that is directly related to disease prevention (all good husbandry techniques are, but this one is massively important). The truth is, many captive reptiles and amphibians fall victim to disease because their keepers don't practice cage-cleaning rituals as often as they should or as efficiently as they should.

I will offer a simple step-by-step cage-cleaning method that has been utilized by a number of keepers, including myself, throughout the years, with great success. You can follow it to the letter or modify it here and there to suit your needs, but it is most important that you *do* keep your pets's tanks clean, because prevention of diseases is a great deal easier than curing them.

1) Remove all the snakes and put them in a secure container. This can be nearly anything suitable, i.e., a plastic shoebox or sweaterbox, a bucket with a locking lid, a large jar, etc. Fill the container with a little water too.

2) Remove all climate-control items, such as lights, heating apparatus, etc.

3) Remove all items from the tank that are washable and reusable and place them in a bucket. This includes gravel, large rocks, and so forth.

4) Remove all disposable items, whatever they may be, and throw them away.

5) Remove all plants, if there are any, and place them in suitable temporary containers.

6) Fill the now-empty tank with a mixture of warm water, dish soap, and a splash of bleach. The bleach is of course the most powerful cleanser and will effectively destroy most any germs that would otherwise threaten your snakes's health. Scrub the tank clean with a plastic pad (not steel wool, for the glass will get badly scratched), paying special attention to the corners, where the glass meets the plastic rim, and other such subtle spots.

7) Empty out the warm water/ soap/bleach mixture and rinse the tank very thoroughly in cold water. Keep rinsing until the effluent is clear and holds no further scent of bleach.

8) Dry the tank thoroughly.

9) Using the same method, now clean all reusable tank items.

10) Now set up the tank again and place the snakes back into it.

Finally, it should be pointed out that there really isn't any need to set a concrete cleaning schedule for yourself; simply tend to the tanks whenever they get dirty.

FEEDING

The keeper of Pine Snakes and their kin is indeed fortunate, for not only are Pine Snakes amazingly hardy animals, but willing and eager feeders that subsist almost entirely on a small mammal diet, i.e., mice and rats.

FOOD ITEMS

Mice and Rats

These are undoubtedly the two items most often offered to captive *Pituophis*. In the wild, the diet of Pine Snakes, as far as eating small mammals is concerned, goes beyond mice and rats and further includes such things as squirrels, voles, shrews, chipmunks, and so on, but for the sake of convenience, a keeper probably will not be offering any of these things.

Mice can be obtained a number of ways, the most obvious being through a pet shop. Virtually any pet shop will carry mice, if not as food items than as pets. Mice are fairly inexpensive and probably will be available in a number of sizes. The smallest size is, of course, the "pinkie," which is sort of a nickname for a newborn mouse. Whether pinkies earned their name from the fact that they slightly resemble the pinky finger on the human hand or because they are very pink in color, I am not sure; but there it is nevertheless. Pinkies make good meals for very young Pine Snakes, as do "fuzzies," which are the next grade up from pinkies. Fuzzies are so called because they are covered lightly with

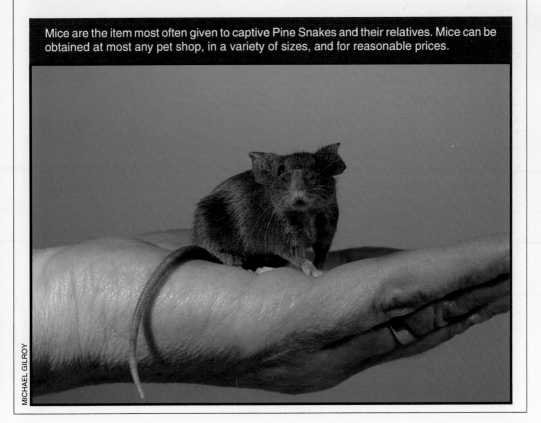

Mice are the item most often given to captive Pine Snakes and their relatives. Mice can be obtained at most any pet shop, in a variety of sizes, and for reasonable prices.

MICHAEL GILROY

MICHAEL GILROY

In the wild, chipmunks are often taken by snakes of the genus *Pituophis*, although there probably aren't a lot of keepers who can (or are willing to) supply chipmunks to their captive snakes! The truth is, Pine Snakes and their relatives will probably go after any small mammals they think they can swallow.

their first hairs. Beyond pinkies and fuzzies, you have subadults, young adults, medium adults, and then the older ones.

If, for some reason, your local pet store doesn't carry mice or, at the very least, doesn't have the sizes you need. You can consider breeding them yourself. Just keep in mind that they can become very pesty to keep on your premises. Further on you will find the information needed. Follow the instructions given and you'll be up to your ears in mice! Another option is to contact one of the many rodent breeders who caters to the needs of those who keep mammal-eating pets such as Pine Snakes. Just so you know what to expect ahead of time, you will not be able to buy only a few dozen mice from these folks; they almost always deal in bulk (any order under one hundred is most unusual). You also have the option of ordering the mice alive or dead and

Rats are a good meal for larger *Pituophis*, and, like mice, they can be obtained at many pet shops, and in a variety of sizes. Be careful, though, that your snakes don't get hooked onto rats—afterwards, some of them might never take mice again!

MICHAEL GILROY

MICHAEL GILROY

Pinkie mice are commonly given to very young *Pituophis*. Pinkie mice are small enough to be taken by any neonatal member of the genus, they form a complete meal, and they can be obtained without too much trouble on the keeper's part.

frozen. I do not wish to make any of this sound discouraging, because it shouldn't be. Ordering bulk quantities of mice has some great advantages, one of which is that it will save you many trips.

If you decide to make an order for, say, one hundred live mice, keep in mind that if they are pinkies or fuzzies, they will not survive long without a mother, so chances are you'll have to either offer them as food right away or freeze them yourself. Adult mice ordered alive, however, will have to be cared for until they are utilized, so keep a tank or two handy so you can house them while they are awaiting sentence.

Frozen mice should be kept in a freezer until needed. Described methods of thawing frozen rodents, or for that matter frozen herp foods of any kind, have been plentiful, but

for the sake of alacrity I will offer only one, that which I have used since the beginning of my keeping days and with continued reliability. Soak the item, whatever it may be, in a container of warm water (not hot, but just as warm as your tap can muster. No need to boil or anything like that). For complete thawing, it should take anywhere from 10 to 40 minutes, depending on the size of the item (a large mouse or rat will obviously take longer to thaw than a pinkie). Once the animal seems limp and flexible (i.e., fully thawed), dry it well with a hand towel and then offer it to your snake(s). Other methods I have heard of involve either the use of a microwave (there seem to be some pretty sick minds out there...) and the concept of leaving the item out to air-thaw in a warm room overnight. The latter method is

W. P. MARA

This is not a pretty sight, but it is fairly typical of how a large *Pituophis* specimen will deal with a food item like the adult rat being taken here. Pine Snakes and their relatives are remarkably strong and will be very violent in their constricting methods. If you have a weak stomach, you may not want to watch something like this. The snake shown is a patternless Northern Pine Snake, *Pituophis melanoleucus melanoleucus.*

acceptable if you have the time and patience, so the choice is yours, but I prefer the soaking method over all else. Either way, the priority is to fully thaw the food item before offering it because a Pine Snake that has swallowed a partially frozen mouse will become very ill.

The final option for maintaining a large mouse supply is to breed them yourself. There are, as with anything else, pros and cons to this endeavor. On the good side, you will have full control of your food stock and thus you will always have a varied

selection to choose from. On the bad side, mice stink to high heaven and the chores involved in their maintenance are more than many people care to deal with. In any case, the decision is purely yours; I will simply offer you the method.

Start off with about five breeding quartets, a quartet being one adult male and three adult females; again, you probably will have to acquire these from a pet shop or rodent breeder. You can tell the sexes apart because the males, quite frankly, have testicles. These can be seen if you allow the mouse to hang by its front legs from a pencil that is being held out horizontally. As the mouse tries to climb and balance itself, its testicles will either bulge out, or, if the mouse is a female, they (obviously) won't! Not a very pleasant (or dignified) moment for the mouse, but that's the way it goes.

Once you have acquired your stock, set them up in 10-gallon tanks. Include into these breeding tanks a water bottle and a bedding of wood shavings. Water bottles can be acquired at any pet store that carries small mammals and wood shavings can be acquired either at the same pet store or at a feed store that stocks horse supplies and so forth. It is important to note that wood shavings of the cedar variety should

not be used because the oils are toxic to snakes. The plain old pine variety will be fine.

Once you have the mice set up in their tank and all ready to go, feed them on a simple diet of bird seed and dry dog food. I am not going to go into which brands are best in the case of either item, but I would like to point out that many other rodent breeders I have spoken with over the years insist that they must only use only the finest bird seed and dry dog food available, plus the addition of any of the various "treat" foods designed for small rodents, whereas I, on the other hand, have always utilized generic bird seed and store-brand dry dog food, and have never experienced any nutritional problems whatsoever. There is a technique

Most squirrel species are small enough, and appealing enough, for snakes in the genus *Pituophis* to go after. It is not at all unusual for a hungry Pine or Gopher Snake to scale a large tree to secure one of these small mammals.

LUCI QUINN

called "gut-loading" that is based on the concept that whatever is in the stomach of your Pine Snake's food will be passed on to the snake itself, and thus it is a good idea to fill the food item with as much beneficial stuff as possible. I agree with this technique and advise its practice, and therefore will say that I do think certain vitamin additives are acceptable when feeding your mice, but only feed such additives to those mice that are you are planning on offering in the very near future; giving supplements to all of your breeder mice all the time can be quite costly.

After your mice are situated in their tanks and are feeding away, you can expect results very quickly. Mice have a most remarkable reproductive system—a healthy female can give birth every 21 days, and, once she gets going, she probably will do just that! The litters will range in size from three or four to about 15. Once the young are born, the mother will pay a great amount of attention to them, laying over her pile and allowing them to feed off her. It is important to remember that you shouldn't really put anymore than three females and a single male in one 10-gallon tank or else you run the risk of fierce competition for food, which, in turn, means if the adults can't find anything to eat, they'll start eating the newborn mice. Sounds gross, I know, but it is still true.

This leads to one other topic—the fact that mice are quite sensitive about their young and seem to really "lose it" when confronted with certain

Facing Page: This young Florida Pine Snake, *Pituophis melanoleucus mugitus*, formerly of the author's private collection, was fairly typical of the Pine Snakes in its captive eating habits—it would very willingly take small mice and tiny birds' eggs. Photo by Mella Panzella.

stimuli. For example, if you reach your hand in and start fooling with a litter of newborn mice, there is a very good chance that, because those mice now have a different smell to them, either their mother, or one of the other adults, will take offense to this new odor and kill the litter off. Conversely, a drippy water bottle (which leads to wet wood shavings) also seems to push adult mice to infanticide, as does a really filthy tank (mouse tanks should be cleaned *at least* once every two weeks). Since I'm not a mouse psychologist I really can't offer any concrete explanations for this awful behavior, but there it is anyway and you should be made aware of it. If you need to take any small mice from a litter, a simple method is by scooping them up with a spoon taped to the end of a stick. I have used this little idea with great success over the years. Beyond that, if the little mouse you have taken is refused by the Pine Snake you offered it to, you can get the mother mouse to accept it back by placing the mouse somewhere else in the tank and covering it up with dirty wood shavings. The "mouse smell" will then return to the little mouse and the mother will dig it up, give it an approving sniff, and then return it to the litter herself.

By keeping a number of breeding tanks going at the same time, you will assure yourself a continual flow of mouse food. In time, you may find you have more mice than you ever dreamed of (if, of course, you do have dreams about such things, in which case you should put this book down and seek professional help). If and when this happens, set up another tank, this one a 20-gallon, and place your surplus mice in there. A very good habit to get into is to save a few of the healthier adults so they can replace the existing breeders when the latter gets too old or fails to produce respectable-sized litters any longer. The average amount of time one can expect a female to continually produce good litters is about one year, although the mice will live a bit longer than that.

Information concerning rats is basically the same as that which I have offered on mice, with only a few subtle differences. As far as breeding rats goes, think of them as nothing more than really big mice. A quartet of rats, for example, will require a 20-gallon tank rather than a 10-gallon. They will also, naturally, require more food and water. Rats are a bit more intelligent than mice and don't seem quite as nervy, so chances are you won't have rats killing off their young half as much as mice do (although that still isn't to say you should go handling rat fuzzies whenever the urge hits you). Also, remember that rat bites really hurt; I once had one latch onto my right forefinger and dig right down to the bone. One last note on the subject of rat breeding—there aren't too many things on Mother Earth that smell worse than captive rats do. Keep em' downwind, if you know what I mean.

Rats also can be bought at many pet stores or in bulk from rodent breeders, but they are, as you might be able to guess, a little more expensive than mice. Since they are larger, they also will be more expensive to ship. Needless to say, adult rats should only be offered to the largest Pine Snakes, and if you are the type who believes in offering food items alive, be sure to stay around for each feeding because large rats can do some serious damage to a snake if they are given the chance. Furthermore, you should remember that many snakes get sort of addicted to rats once they have been given

Although the snakes of the genus *Pituophis* seem willing to eat just about any small mammals that are placed in front of them, a keeper will only be able to supply a handful of items. The mole that is being checked out by this Gopher Snake, *Pituophis catenifer*, for example, may be a good meal for the snake, but the idea obtaining moles on a regular basis probably isn't very practical. Photo by K. H. Switak.

them on a regular basis, so perhaps it is best that you stick to mice for the staple diet and only offer rats occasionally. If you have no problem supplying rats on a constant basis, than perhaps this will be of no concern to you, but if not, then be careful. I once had a snake that would take mice religiously, until one day a friend of mine, who was temporarily housing it at his place, decided to give it a few rat pups. After that, the snake wouldn't even look at

consequently, their appeal to Pine Snakes. Freshly laid eggs are, of course the best, as the scent is quite strong. Most bird breeders, and virtually all farmers, will be glad to sell any eggs they may have lying around, and for a fair price. As I mentioned before, birds's eggs are a good meal for a Pine Snake and should be offered when possible. It should be pointed out, however, that they really cannot be considered a staple food. They are a great supplement and are highly recommended, but they do not make up a complete nutritional picture.

Birds themselves are also an excellent meal for Pine Snakes, and they too can be purchased through a bird breeder or farmer. Needless to say, birds are not the Pine Snake food item to go to a pet shop for.

mice, and it was all downhill from there...

Birds and Birds' Eggs

Two other items often taken by wild Pine Snakes and their kin are birds and their eggs. Neither of these are particularly difficult for the ambitious keeper to acquire and both make a good meal.

To begin with, let me point out that Pine Snakes are not going to accept eggs that have been store-bought and doled out from a carton; even snakes aren't that dumb. If you really want to feed your Pine Snakes birds' eggs, you are going to have to contact a bird breeder or go to a farm and get the aforementioned eggs fresh. Once all that processing and chilling takes place, the eggs lose their scent and,

If you wanted to supply a real treat for your Pine Snakes, you could go to a local farmer and purchase a few chickens. Most snakes of the genus *Pituophis* like small chickens and will take them without fuss. If you do decide to do this, see if you can get some fresh eggs as well; Pine Snakes and their kin seem to enjoy those too.

FROM *POULTRY AS A HOBBY*

Even if you had the money to buy finches or budgies every week, who'd want to? Quail, chicks, guinea hens, pheasants, etc.; these are the birds you want. They too will be very inexpensive and can be obtained with some regularity.

Vitamin Supplements

There have been a number of products designed explicitly for the pet industry to aid the keeper in the efficient maintenance of their animal's nutritional standing. More precisely, some of these products were designed with herptiles in mind, and one of them is the vitamin supplement.

Vitamin supplements come in two forms—powder and liquid. There are also two ways in which to administer these vitamins—through tube-feeding or along with a food item. Since it is my belief that tube-feeding of any kind is an act of desperation on the keeper's part, and since tube-feeding

of any kind poses some dangers, I will say that only the latter option, including vitamins with a food item, is sensible. Powders can either be sprinkled onto a dead item or added into a live item's food (as discussed earlier). Liquids can also be poured onto a dead item or, again, included in a live item's food. Both liquids and powders can be purchased at your local pet shop and should be used in conjunction with Pine Snakes and their kin about every tenth feeding, and in small doses. Remember, vitamins of this kind are only a supplement and should not be over-used. If they are, hypervitaminosis (an over-abundance of vitamins) will be the result, possibly killing your pet(s).

HOW MUCH FOOD AND HOW OFTEN?

The question of how much food a Pine Snake should be given, and how often it should be fed, can be puzzling

Quail and quails' eggs make a good meal for Pine Snakes and other *Pituophis*. Although most quail are sold as pets (and at prices one wouldn't want to spend on a food item!), some of the lesser varieties can be obtained inexpensively enough if you can find a society or private breeder.

KEITH HINDWOOD

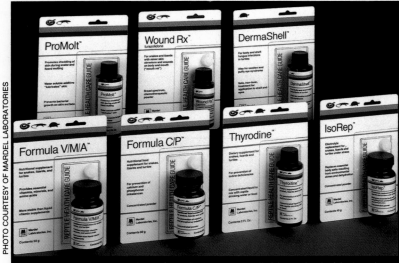

PHOTO COURTESY OF MARDEL LABORATORIES

There are quite a number of products now available to the hobbyist who wants to take minor medical matters into his or her own hands. It should be pointed out, however, that preventive medicine is the only form of herptile medicine a layman should practice on a regular basis; leave the complicated matters to the veterinarians.

to some keepers. Just because Pine Snakes and their relatives are voracious eaters doesn't mean you should feed them until they pop. Overfeeding is just as dangerous as underfeeding, so be aware of the fact that there is both a right and wrong way of going about this.

Depending on the size of your snake, you should give it a good-sized meal every five days. Of course, there are many reasons why a Pine Snake may not stick to this schedule; it is idealistic rather than realistic, but a goal nevertheless. If the snake is in a shed phase, if it is gravid, or if it just feels like fasting for a while, it may not eat at all. If this is the case, don't worry. There's a rule of thumb to remember concerning snakes and their little fasting phases—if the snake is not losing any weight or otherwise seems to be suffering from its sudden unwillingness to eat, then don't worry about it. Again, the ideal interval between feedings is five days.

Since I used the phrase "good-sized meal," I suppose I should take a

moment out to define it. In my opinion, based on my experiences with *Pituophis*, I would say, for a newborn specimen, five pinkies or three fuzzies; for a sub-adult, two adult mice; and for really large adults, two rats or six mice. From these estimations, you can easily ascertain the needs of any specimens that lie between the categories given.

OFFERING THE FOOD—ALIVE OR DEAD?

This probably has been one of the most hotly debated issues in the world of herpetoculture. What is better, giving a Pine Snake its food alive or dead?

Most keepers seem to think dead is best. If asked for a percentage estimation, I would say at least 75% of all advanced keepers of Pine Snakes and their kin offer foods dead.

But my personal preference is live. Don't get me wrong here—this is purely a personal preference and should not weigh on whatever decision you choose to make..The reason I prefer live food is because I like to make my snakes work for their meals. Unless the enclosures you keep your Pine Snakes in are remarkably large, chances are the snakes will not get the opportunity to exercise much. Therefore, giving them food they have to chase around and kill will get them moving once and a while.

On the other hand, there are of course the dangers of a live item turning against a snake and injuring it. It has been known to happen, and on more than one occasion. When you feed a Pine Snake a live food item, you really should stay and watch what happens; the problem is, not all keepers always have the time to do this.

Thus, you now see the advantage of offering dead food—the feedings don't have to be supervised. The food can be left in the tank overnight, which is good because some snakes, although they may be hungry, will either eat only in the dark, only during night hours, or only when there are no humans around to watch them. The only true disadvantage to feeding dead food is, what if the snake doesn't take it? What do you do with a thawed rat that doesn't get eaten? You can only re-freeze it so many times. This is one more consideration to make.

Overall, the choice is purely yours; I have simply offered points for and against both options.

FORCE-FEEDING

And herein lies the final topic concerning the feeding of Pine Snakes and their kin—forcing them to take food when they've decided they're not going to do it themselves.

It is important to first point out that I consider this to be purely an emergency option, and so should you. Force-feeding is not only remarkably stressful for a snake, but it does indeed pose certain health dangers as well. The techniques involved are very delicate and should be handled only by those with dexterity, nerve, patience, and, hopefully, experience.

There are two types of force-feeding—feeding liquid through a tube, and feeding solids with the aid of forceps.

To give liquid feedings, you must first acquire a force-feeding syringe. These can be obtained through pet stores that stock a respectable amount of herpetocultural supplies, or you can try a drug store. After that, you will have to find some thin plastic tubing to be attached to the syringe's end. This is the tubing that will be run down the snake's throat, so be sure there is a good length of it—about two feet. Why so much? Because it will allow you the freedom you'll need to manipulate things. If the tube is too short, the syringe will hang down as you try to work the tube into the snake's mouth, and the weight will work against you. Also, be sure to cut the end of the tube at a fairly sharp angle so it will be easier to slip between the snake's jaws.

The liquid mixture should consist of some lean hamburger meat, a raw egg or two, and a sprinkling of vitamin powder, blended into a liquid in an ordinary kitchen blender, and then run through a strainer (to remove all that excess stuff that gets hidden in meat these days). Remember to give this liquid warm or, at the very least, room temperature. If you give it cold you're going to have a

Facing Page: This photo (taken by Robert T. Zappalorti, who has devoted much of his life to reptile and amphibian conservation) shows a Northern Pine Snake, *Pituophis melanoleucus melanoleucus*, scaling a tree in the New Jersey Pine Barrens. Many snakes of the genus *Pituophis* will do this to secure squirrels or field mice, but others will go so far as to raid birds' nests, taking not only the birds, but the eggs as well.

very sick snake on your hands (or, more precisely, in your hands).

Now for the procedure. Again, remember, you need a lot of nerve, a bit of nimbleness, and preferably someone nearby to hold the snake's body still if you are working with a large specimen. First, fill the syringe with the liquid mixture and then coat the end of the tube with some inert lubricant (I like to use vegetable oil). Then, holding the snake's head firmly, wiggle the point of the tube until you can get it between its jaws. Once it is in, gently slide it down until you've gone about one-fifth of the way down. It is important at this point to keep in mind that if you don't push the tube down far enough, there is a very good chance any liquid you force down will simply leak out the sides of the snake's mouth. Gently press down on the plunger of the syringe so the liquid goes in slowly. Once you have finished, pull the tube back out with equal gentleness. The amount given will, again, depend on the size of the snake. The amount should equal about two-thirds of what the animal would take in normal food, and the intervals between force-feeding should, again, be about every five days.

In the case of solid foods, the best items to use are either strips of raw beef sprinkled with vitamin powder or actual dead food items sprinkled with the same. From here on I will refer to both of these collectively as "item" so I don't have to keep specifying.

Again, you have to first dip the item in lubricant, and then busy yourself with the opening of the snake's jaws. This can be done quite simply by prying them back with a popsicle stick (also coated with lubricant so as not to damage the snake's mouth). Once you've got the jaws open, slip the food item in and remove the popsicle stick. Then, grab the item on either side with long forceps (about 12 in/30 cm, if you can find a pair—call a surgical supply house; that's where I got mine), and just push the item down. Once it has disappeared from the forefront of the jaws, slide the tweezers back out, close them, and use the point the push the item further down. Once you have gone as far with that as possible, close the snake's mouth and use your other hand to gently massage the item down even further. All this will make it that much more difficult for the snake to regurgitate the meal. After you are through with the force-feeding, place the snake *very gently* back into its enclosure, cover the enclosure with a towels or something (because at this point the snake will be massively stressed), and then leave it alone for a day or so.

The keeper of any snake of the genus *Pituophis* usually needn't worry about his or her snake's appetite; most *Pituophis* will probably end up eating them out of house and home! The snake shown here, taking a medium-sized rat, is an albino Sonoran Gopher Snake, *Pituophis catenifer affinis*.

W. P. MARA

BREEDING

Since Pine Snakes and the rest of the *Pituophis* gang are so wonderfully popular, it goes without saying that they are captive-bred like mad. Although they still aren't as popular as, say, the kingsnakes and Milk Snakes (genus *Lampropeltis*), the rat snakes (genus *Elaphe*), or the boids (boas and pythons), they are undoubtedly set firmly in fourth place (in the snake world, that is), so that's not so bad. Being a massive *Pituophis* fanatic myself, I still wonder why they're not first, but then I am partial to Scarlet Snakes, *Cemophora coccinea*, so it already goes without saying that my judgment is somewhat questionable.

In this chapter you will be exposed to all relevant facets of the breeding of the Pine Snakes and their relatives, which will hopefully give you enough base knowledge to breed them yourself. In truth, they really aren't difficult to breed at all, which doubtless is one reason why they're so sought after.

SEXUAL DIMORPHISM

How could you possibly expect two Pine Snakes to breed if you weren't even sure they were male and female? Don't worry; telling the sexes apart is not particularly difficult.

What you need to do first is purchase something called a sexing probe. A sexing probe is nothing more than a small, thin rod of stainless steel (usually) with a tiny ball tip. This tip is inserted into the snake's cloaca, nearer to the sides than to the middle, and then gently slid toward the posterior. The idea is to see how far the probe will go. If it hits an obstacle after only a few scales, chances are it is a female. If it goes in about six to eight scales, chances are

it is a male.

Probes can be purchased from some general pet stores and from petshops that specialize in herp supplies. The probes usually come in sets of three and are reasonably priced. You should remember to always wipe a probe down with some alcohol before using it, and further coat the tip with some inert lubricant before sticking it into a snake. The procedure is quite delicate and should only be performed by someone with a steady hand and, at the very least, a good amount of knowledge toward what he or she is doing. If you stick a probe in too hard, you could very easily damage a snake, rendering it useless as a breeder. If you do not feel you have the aptitude to probe a Pine Snake, bring it to someone who does and watch them. Eventually you'll get the hang of it.

THE FIRST STEP—HIBERNATION

Captive snakes of the genus *Pituophis* cannot be induced to breed unless they first undergo a brief period of artificial hibernation. Many keepers have claimed to own specimens that have bred repeatedly without ever being hibernated, and I have no doubts that these claims are true, but I prefer not to take such chances. Hibernation, you see, is an essential part of the reproductive cycle of Pine Snakes and their kin in the wild. During hibernation, the reproductive hormones are sort of regenerated and recharged for the next season. Most snakes that do not hibernate will not breed, or, at the very least, may actually copulate, but the eggs they produce will be infertile. I would guess this is the case at least 70% of the time, even with specimens

that have spent their entire lives in captivity, so do yourself a favor and hibernate your *Pituophis*. Why take chances?

The first consideration is deciding which specimens can and cannot be hibernated. Hibernation, keep in mind, is a massive strain on a snake, so those that are ill in health should not be submitted to this process. Any snakes that have been feeding poorly or have definite ailments should be kept warm during the winter months and not hibernated until the next season (assuming, of course, they are in better shape by that time).

Once you have chosen your best stock, the next step is setting up the hibernaculum. This can be just about anything. I usually use a few 20-gallon tanks filled with about a three-inch layer of sterile potting soil. I find that snakes like soil and will burrow into it. Also, include a small waterbowl and, of course, a tank top that fits tightly. Remember, snakes still move about during hibernation and will still grab the opportunity to escape.

The location of the hibernaculum is unimportant as long as it is in a place where you can get to it when you need to, and where the correct temperature can be maintained (more on that in a moment).

Now, you have to prepare your snakes for the hibernation period. The key idea here is to empty out their systems completely. Two weeks before you plan to hibernate them, stop feeding them completely. During the last week, give them all a bath in

Facing Page: In the wild, *Pituophis* mothers will lay their eggs in an underground chamber, then remain with the eggs for a few days after. Ultimately, however, they will abandon the clutch and perform no further maternal functions. The snake shown is a Northern Pine Snake, *Pituophis melanoleucus melanoleucus*. Photo by Robert T. Zappalorti.

warm water for about two hours each day. This will help flush out all of the remaining wastes that might be floating around in their system.

When the big day arrives, place them into their hibernaculum and drop their temperature slowly, i.e., about five degrees everyday. The temperature you're looking for for the *Pituophis* group is somewhere in the neighborhood of around 52°F/11°C. This, in my experience, has always proved itself the ideal number for all species involved (even the Mexican ones). Those Pine Snakes that occur far north (like the Northern Pine Snake, *Pituophis melanoleucus melanoleucus*, for example), can go down to as low as 43°F/6°C, but that's really cutting it close. Use the number I gave the first time and you'll have no problems.

The duration of hibernation can be anywhere from six to ten weeks, but I have always just played it in the middle and used eight. This seems to be more than sufficient for all species involved. Any less than that and I think you're asking for trouble, but anything over ten weeks seems excessive. During this time, be sure to check on the snakes at least once a week, changing their waterbowl each time. Beyond that, do not disturb them in any way, for the procedure will be stressful enough without you sticking your face in every other minute. The hibernation chamber should be totally dark, and quiet, and should be able to maintain the temperature required. If the temperature fluctuates a little, that's okay, but don't let it fluctuate too much. If it goes to high, the snakes will linger in and out of hibernation and this may seriously endanger their health. If it goes too low, you may end up with a "snakesickle" rather than a potential breeder. If you think you may experience the latter scenario, do yourself a favor and place a small cube heater into the hibernation chamber, along with a portable thermostat.

After the hibernation period has ended, bring the snakes' temperature back up to normal in the same way you dropped it—slowly (about five degrees per day). Afterwards, place the snakes back into their respective enclosures (keep the males and the females separated until you are ready to breed them) and leave them alone for three more days. They will be disoriented and in no mood to do much else during this time except recover. After that, you can begin feeding them again.

MATING

Once your snakes have been hibernated and have begun feeding, it is time to pair them up and let breeding commence. I have always placed the females into the males's enclosures and I suggest you do the same. Only place one female in with one male at a time. Pine Snakes and their kin have displayed male combat rituals in the wild on more than one occasion, but in captivity it seems this act does nothing to further stimulate a breeding response, so don't bother even trying to encourage it.

Actual copulation will not take long—perhaps up to three hours at the utmost. It usually only lasts about 20 to 40 minutes on average. You can witness this fascinating event if you wish, but be sure to keep your distance. An interested male will rub himself against the female and ride along her back, trying to wrap his tail around hers in an attempt to line up their cloacas (sometimes he will do this with great aggressiveness). If the female is receptive, she will lift her tail and allow him to insert one of his two hemipenes. Once the hemipenis is in place, the male may suddenly stop his restless motions and the two may just sit there for a while, literally motionless. Eventually the female may get tired of the inertia and begin to move off, at which time the male may very likely bite down on her head or just slightly posterior to it. If you witness this, don't be alarmed; it is quite normal. Unlike many other animals, Pine Snakes and their kin are not very violent with each other during copulation.

Once the pair are done copulating and they have separated, you can take the female back out of the enclosure and try putting her back in again in week or so. The more times you breed them, the better the chances that she will be fertile.

CARE OF GRAVID FEMALES

Once a female Pine Snake is gravid, she will undergo a few physiological changes, and these changes will manifest themselves on the outside in ways a keeper will be able to notice. For one, she may become a little more aggressive towards people. If this is the case, simply give the snake a little more privacy and, whatever you do, don't handle it. Also, you may notice a distinct reduction in her food intake, but this too is normal. Fasting and pregnancy are common bedfellows with many creatures, humans included. Not all pregnant snakes will lose their appetite, but many do. All in all, a pregnant Pine Snake should be given as much food as she's willing to take (within reason, of course), given lots of privacy, and kept warm. Do not stress her.

EGGLAYING

The average gestation period for a snake in the genus *Pituophis is* around 70 days, give or take. Once the female starts looking really plump, you know the time is drawing near. It is at this time that you are

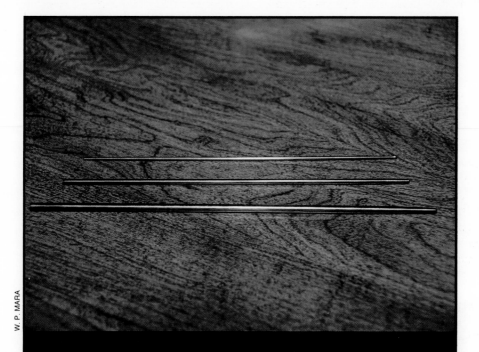

W. P. MARA

Above: Stainless steel sexing probes usually are sold in sets of three, as shown above. Using a sexing probe is the best way for an ordinary snake keeper to determine the sex of his or her specimens. **Below:** An albino Florida Pine Snake, *Pituophis melanoleucus mugitus*. This animal is a monument to today's captive-breeding efforts and is undoubtedly one of the most stunning examples of the genus *Pituophis*.

W. P. MARA

going to have to provide her with a nesting box.

Nesting boxes need not be particularly fancy. I have always used a plastic shoebox with a large entrance hole cut through the lid. I line the box with about a two-inch layer of heavily granular vermiculite, moistened to the point where it is damp, but not wet. With really large Pine Snakes, you may want to promote your nesting box to a plastic sweaterbox rather than the smaller shoebox. Leave the nesting box in the female's tank and let her slither into it when she's ready. When your instincts tell you the day is near, check the box frequently to see if you have any eggs yet. Once they have been laid, carefully (and I mean carefully) remove the female from the nesting box if she has not left it on her own. Then, remove the box and it will now shift its purpose from being

the nesting box to being the incubation chamber.

EGG INCUBATION

The eggs of the Pine Snakes and their relatives can be laid in two ways—in a cluster or separately. Of course, the latter is preferable. Why? Because if you have a bunch of eggs all stuck together and one of them goes bad, it may infect the other eggs. If you happen to be around when your snake is laying, try your best to keep the eggs apart, if possible. Remember that they will dry and stick very quickly; if this happens, don't attempt to pull them apart or you will very probably damage them. Also, it is crucial to keep in mind that snake eggs should always be left in the exact position in which they were laid. If you think you will have to move them for whatever reason, mark the tops of the eggs with a water-

Sphagnum moss is one of the two most effective substrates used for artificially incubating *Pituophis* eggs (the other is vermiculite). The snakes shown are Northern Pine Snakes, *Pituophis melanoleucus melanoleucus.*

W. P. MARA

The moment every captive snake breeder waits for—a healthy neonate sticking its head out of a freshly cut shell. Some snakes may remain in their shells for a day or two after making this initial incision. If this happens, just leave them alone; they'll come out eventually. The snake shown is a Northern Pine Snake, *Pituophis melanoleucus melanoleucus*.

W. P. MARA

based magic marker.

Now that you have the eggs in their incubation box, cover the entrance hole that the snake slid through so to retain the moisture. Furthermore, drape a few pieces of moistened sphagnum moss over the eggs as an added medium. I have begun using this vermiculite/sphagnum moss coupling very recently and have been very pleased with the results. The incubation medium should be checked every third day to assure that it is still moist, and if it begins to dry, use a spray mist bottle to wet it again. Be careful not to wet the eggs themselves, as that could be dangerous. To moisten the sphagnum drapery, simply lift it out, spray it lightly, then place it back in. The ideal incubation temperature is somewhere around 75°F/24°C, but there is a large gradient in either direction. The number given, however, is ideal.

HATCHING TIME

Incubation for Pine Snakes and their relatives lasts about 75 days, give or take a few. When hatching time draws near, be sure the incubation box top is on tight or the snakes will just crawl right out.

You won't have too much trouble figuring out when the snakes have emerged—you'll see, at the very least, their little snouts sticking up out of the slits they made in their eggs. If the urge to yank the top off the incubation box and pull the snakes from their eggs swells up inside you, squelch it; the neonates will come out in their own time. When they do, you'll notice the umbilical cord still attached to their bellies and running back into the shells. Do not cut this, or the snake may die. Let it dry up and fall off on its own. The only thing you can do until the snakes have completely emerged from their shell and lost their umbilical cords is wait. If any eggs haven't hatched but still look good (white and whole rather than yellowish and caved-in), keep them around until you are sure they are spoiled. Snake eggs often do not hatch all at the same time.

CARE OF THE NEONATES

After the young have left their eggs and are free-moving, remove them into their own enclosure. Since Pine Snakes and their relatives are not really cannibalistic, the young can be housed together with little chance of mishap. This is not to say it *never* happens, but only rarely at best, and I am only saying this as a precaution; I have never in my life seen a snake in the genus *Pituophis* eat another snake. The enclosure need not be

If you have the land space and feel like going to the trouble, you can always provide a group of pregnant mothers with the room to dig their own nesting burrows so they can lay their eggs similar to how they would lay them naturally. Shown is a Northern Pine Snake, *Pituophis melanoleucus melanoleucus*, going into her nesting den in the New Jersey Pine Barrens.

ROBERT T. ZAPPALORTI

ROBERT T. ZAPPALORTI

In the wild, albino snakes are a rarity; even those that are born to nature don't live long because their obvious coloring makes them an easy target for predators. Thanks to the legion of captive snake breeders, however, albino snakes of many types, including most of the species of *Pituophis*, are now commercially available. Snake shown is an albino Bullsnake, *Pituophis sayi*.

Albino Northern Pine Snakes, *Pituophis melanoleucus melanoleucus*, have made a small splash in the herpetocultural hobby. Interestingly, the specimen shown here was the one that started that particular bloodline. It is an adult female, found in the New Jersey Pine Barrens in the mid-1980's, and is still alive and well, and breeding, today.

elaborate; refer to the housing chapter in this book for proper procedure.

Once the young are situated, you can begin feeding them after their first shed. This should occur no more than ten days after hatching, usually sooner. Newborn *Pituophis* should be given pinkie mice, or, for big young, fuzzy mice, with the occasional vitamin supplement. Beyond that, the rodent diet can be the staple diet throughout their lives. The young will be very feisty during their first year and will probably hiss, rattle their tails, snap out, and display all sorts of other childish behavior, so you should probably handle them as frequently as possible to get them calmed down. This way, their wonderful dispositions won't carry over into their adulthood. The bite of a neonatal *Pituophis* is virtually ignorable; even the best shots will only draw a speckle of blood or two, but rarely even that. In fact, once a newborn has been hefted into the human hand, chances are it will not bite at all. It seems they just don't care for the initial grasping, but then that's to be expected.

THREE COMMON DISEASES

DYSECDYSIS (SHEDDING PROBLEMS)

One of the more common problems encountered by captive snakes, bad shedding can be the result of many things, such as a tank that is too dry, a tank that lacks a waterbowl (for the snake to bathe in) or a rock (as a rough surface to begin a shed on), a snake that is suffering some other ailment, etc. The point is, a bad shed can develop into real trouble later on, so you should know how to deal with it immediately.

Firstly, the ideal shedding is one that comes off in one long, complete piece. Sometimes a shed will come off in a few large parcels, but even this is not cause for alarm on the keeper's part; as long as it *all comes off*, that's what you're hoping for.

When it doesn't, you should act immediately. Start off with easy solutions—first, soak the snake in warm water and try peeling the old skin off while the snake is soaking. If that doesn't work, try dabbing the areas of stuck-on shed with mineral oil. You may have to pry the skin away with either your fingernail or a pair of tweezers. This can be a tricky affair, so if you don't have a steady hand, find someone who does.

Finally, if all else fails, contact your vet, who may request that you bring the snake in. You're main concern is something called the brille, or eye cap. That, obviously, is the part of the shed that gets stuck to the snake's eyes. If the brilles don't come off, the snake could suffer a secondary infection which, in a worst-case scenario, could result in blindness.

TICKS AND MITES

Ticks and mites are undoubtedly the most common ectoparasites found on captive snakes. Each one can cause serious problems if left untreated, but, fortunately, each can also be treated with relative ease (unless, of course, the invasion has already gotten way out of hand).

Mites can be noticed easily enough—you will see these each about the size of a printed period, crawling all over the body of your snake. They seem to congregate very often at the animal's head, but in truth they could be found anywhere on the body. If you really want to get ambitious, you could wait

In severe cases of dysecdysis (bad shedding), the eye of a snake will actually regress into the skull, and when the infection finally clears up, the snake's vision may or may not return. The specimen shown is the same albino Northern Pine Snake, *Pituophis melanoleucus melanoleucus*, depicted on the preceding page.

W. P. MARA

until the night hours, then abruptly turn on a light; mites are nocturnal creatures, so this will be the easiest time to catch them in action. During the day, they will be hiding between the snake's scales or in the substrate; during the night, however, they will expose themselves.

The best way to deal with a mite infestation is to take a small piece of pest strip (about 2 in/5 cm square), place it in a small plastic container that has a few dozen small holes drilled into it, and place it into the infected snake's quarantine enclosure for about five days. Provide no waterbowl during this time because the water will be tainted by the effects of the strip. After five days, remove the strip, put the waterbowl back in, wait five more days, and then repeat

the process to kill off any newly hatched mites. And, needless to say, give the infected snake's original enclosure a thorough cleaning.

With ticks, you don't really have to worry too much about being attacked by an army; ticks usually operate in small numbers; say, three to five. If you see a tick (which is easier than seeing a mite because ticks are considerably larger and don't hide during the day), don't just grab it and pull; that may cause the tick's head to break off and remain in the snake, which will cause more problems later on.

First, grab the tick with thumb and forefinger and give it a gentle tug. If that doesn't pull it off, light a match, blow it out, and then immediately apply it to the tick. If the creature

The ideal shedding is one that comes off in one smooth, solid piece, although one that breaks up into three or four large pieces isn't all that harmful either. The point is, *all* the skin must come off eventually. Snake shown is a Northern Pine Snake, *Pituophis melanoleucus melanoleucus*.

ROBERT T. ZAPPALORTI

During the early stages of ecdysis (shedding), a snake's eyes will cloud over and become milky in appearance. This condition sometimes is also termed "opacity." The snake shown is a Black Pine Snake, *Pituophis melanoleucus lodingi*.

K. H. SWITAK

still doesn't let go, dab it with either a drop of rubbing alcohol, or, in more severe cases, cover the tick with a wad of petroleum jelly. The jelly should cut off the tick's oxygen to the point where the parasite will let go of the snake willingly. Once the tick has been removed, swab the remaining wound with hydrogen peroxide twice a day until the infection clears up, which it should in about a week.

MOUTH ROT (INFECTIOUS STOMATITIS)

Mouth rot is one of the most common physical diseases that attacks captive snakes. The bad news is, it can be fatal if given the chance. The causes are multiple, but the most common one, at least for captive snakes, is a severe lack of vitamin C. The signs of this disease are hard to miss—the snake will have trouble closing its mouth, the tissues around the gums will appear discolored and swollen, and, in the later stages, the snake's teeth will become loose and might even fall out. Needless to say, the animal will not be too thrilled at the idea of eating during this time, and will sit motionless (although

some snakes have a tendency to sit with their heads submerged in the waterbowl in an attempt to lessen the pain). If the problem grows too far out of hand, the infection will spread down the esophagus, into the stomach, and the snake will eventually die.

However, it is not all that tough to treat and cure mouth rot (provided, of course, you get to it in time). What a keeper needs to do is swab the infected areas with either a 3 % solution of hydrogen peroxide, or a slightly diluted solution of the mouthwash called "Listerine." Both of these methods have proven themselves effective over the years, and thus are recommended. The treatment should be performed at least two times a day for about five days, then once a day for the next two or three. Once you see signs of recovery, you can gradually lessen the frequency of treatments accordingly. If the problem does not improve within a week, call a vet. Beyond that, up the animal's vitamin C intake either by sprinkling vitamin C powder onto the food items, or by force-feeding a diluted vitamin liquid mixture.

MISCELLANEOUS TOPICS

ACQUISITION

Since the hobby of herpetology is going through such a "hot" phase at the moment (and one that looks as though it has no plans of cooling down), there are a number of ways an interested enthusiast can acquire specimens for his or her collection, but the easiest, most common, and most sensible, is through a pet store.

Since pet stores make a point of making money, they will naturally only offer those animals that they think they can sell without too much trouble. Fortunately, the snakes of the genus *Pituophis* fall into this sought-after category. If the pet store nearest to you carries reptiles and amphibians of any kind, chances are they will carry a Pine Snake or one of its relatives. Even if the store doesn't have any *Pituophis* at that particular moment, it is very likely such an animal can be ordered.

When you finally find a pet store that has a Pine Snake or one of its relatives, don't just bring it up to the counter and pay for it; make sure the animal is in good health first, otherwise you may be sorely disappointed; some pet stores do not have any type of refund policy, so be careful. I do not wish to say every pet store in the world carries a legion of sick and dying animals, for that is totally untrue. It is my belief, in fact, that every pet store certainly *wants* to offer animals that are in the best possible condition, but the truth is, this is not always the case; it's no one's fault, it just happens. Any animal that has gone through the rigors of travel or has spent the last two months in a distributor's warehouse will be a little weathered; if any of them came into the situation

In certain areas of California, there are populations of the Gopher Snake, *Pituophis catenifer*, that have longitudinal dorsal stripes rather than the normal blotches. Snakes of this variety also are commercially bred and can be acquired through the proper channels.

already ill, then they will be even more so by the time they reach the pet store. It is your job as an intelligent consumer to do a quick on-the-spot health check to assure yourself a good value.

First, ask a store employee if you can see the snake eat. Keep in mind that if the snake has already eaten recently or if it is in the middle of a shed phase, it may not want to eat. If this is the case, pass on the purchase and come back in a few days. It has always been my policy not to purchase a snake whose appetite I am not sure is wholly reliable.

Secondly, inspect the animal's physical features, looking for the obvious signs of ill health. Is it scrawny? Can you see a rib cage? Does it have mites or ticks? Any open wounds? (Remember that some snakes will boast a few scars. Unless these are really large, chances are they should not be a cause for concern). Look around the head; how do the eyes look? Are they clear and sharp, or swollen and/or crusty? How does the snake's breathing sound? Silent, or heavy and labored? How does the snake react to your touch? With liveliness or with lethargy? If it is the latter case, something's wrong. Pine Snakes and their kin, while fairly resistant to biting, do not like being poked or prodded. If you jab a finger onto the snake's tail and it doesn't jump as if it had been given a jolt of electric shock, then that snake is probably not in great shape.

Once you're sure the snake is in good health and is eating well, then you can make your purchase.

A lot of enthusiasts wonder about the true difference in quality between wild-caught snakes and those that have been cultured in captivity. The fact is, there *is* a great amount of difference. For example, many wild-caught specimens have trouble adapting to captive life and will not eat, will suffer severe stress, and may already have a number of ailments when they enter your collection. With captive-bred stock, these problems are rarely encountered.

The real problem is telling wild-caught snakes from those that have been captive-bred; sometimes it is very difficult. Generally speaking, if the snakes are very young, it can be next to impossible, but adults, however, are a different story—wild-caught adult snakes usually boast a few "battle scars" here and there as a result of their years in the wild. Captive-bred adults rarely, if ever, have any morphological imperfections. Also, captive-bred specimens tend to respond better to human company, which is also a symptom of never having been exposed to the "wild life." (Animals that are used to living in forests and prairies tend not to have had a lot of exposure to humankind.) Finally, you can always just simply ask the pet store people if the animals they are selling are captive-bred or not. (You really don't have to worry about getting a dishonest answer because there are many breeders who supply pet stores with quality animals; reptile and amphibian breeding is a popular hobby these days.)

Also, I'd like to point out that I believe almost every single *Pituophis* variety is being captive-bred by somebody (you have to figure out which variety you want and then find the appropriate breeder), and there are even a load of gorgeous color varieties that can't even be found in the wild, not to mention a number of albinos (the albino Florida Pine Snakes, *Pituophis melanoleucus mugitus*, which are fairly new to the commercial market, are absolutely breathtaking), so you have a great many snakes to choose from.

The "patternless" Pine Snake has become something of a rave among *Pituophis* enthusiasts. Most are Florida Pine Snakes, *Pituophis melanoleucus mugitus*, that have been selectively breed to lose their light brown dorsal blotching.

HANDLING

Many keepers like to handle their snakes. I am not of this nature, but I do understand the appeal—snakes are fascinating animals to look at and to feel as they glide through your palms and run across your shoulders.

So, are Pine Snakes and their kin really "handleable" animals? The answer is yes, they are. I did indeed state in an earlier chapter that they are fairly temperamental and will hiss, rear back, and even lunge, but usually this is only a bluff, and even when it isn't, I have found that *once you get them in your hands, they seem to lose all desire to bite.* There is, of course, always the chance of getting struck when handling a snake, so using caution should be standard procedure.

But, if you have a Pine Snake that you know to be somewhat temperamental, you really should spend some time handling it, if for no

other reason then because a snake that is that tense will be extremely stressed, and stress weighs heavily on captive snakes. All you really need to do with a nasty snake is spend about an hour a day, for about two months, handling it. Grab it first by the head, then give the body as much support as possible, letting go of the head only when you feel the snake has calmed down enough not to strike. Allow it to go pretty much where it wishes, keeping in mind that you should still hold it firmly enough that it doesn't get away from you! If you are really that worried about getting bitten, wear a pair of rubber kitchen gloves. Not only do these gloves protect you from the bites, but snakes seem to find them horrible in taste and will learn that much quicker not to strike. It has been my firm belief that even the most irascible snake can be tamed, with time and patience.

KEEPING RECORDS

Any serious and efficient herpetoculturist keeps records. You never know when you might have to refer back to some tiny bit of information that seemed insignificant at the time of its occurrence, only to become massively important later on. A lot of information can be considered important—feedings, sheddings, defecations, vomiting, matings, etc. Anything that a snake does that you think might be noteworthy you should record.

There are a lot of ways one can keep records. One is simply through the use of a notebook. Another method, one that is quite convenient and easy, is to use a micro-cassette recorder. Finally, I have always been fond of those giant desk calendars with big blocks for each date, each block conveniently having a few lines to write on. Instead of placing it on a desk, however, I would tack it to a wall, and then tape a pencil to a string and dangle it nearby. Whenever anything happened, I just walked over and scratched in a little note like "Pine Snake, 2 mice," which obviously meant my Pine Snake had eaten two mice that day. At the end of each month, I would tear the sheet off, fold it up neatly, and file it away. Looking back at all the data I gathered through the years, I'm glad I went to the trouble.

BITES

In the unfortunate event that you get bitten by a Pine Snake or one of its relatives, what should you do? Relax. Snakes of the genus *Pituophis* are, as many people already know, non-venomous, so the worst damage will be a little blood. Even the largest specimens won't do much more than tear the skin. If this happens, simply swab the wound with a little hydrogen peroxide, then cover it up with a light dressing. Then, read the section on handling so you don't get bit again!

FARING IN CAPTIVITY

So, how well do Pine Snakes and their kin fare in captivity? Very well, actually. They are, in truth, among the hardiest serpents one could ever hope to find. They have an average life span of about 15 years (in the wild, that is, although with first-rate care there isn't any reason why they shouldn't be able to live that long in captivity, either) and captive-bred specimens seem perfectly content with captive life. Pine Snakes and their kin are excellent eaters and have a good constitution, unlike some snakes that seem as fragile as porcelain dolls. One point, however, is that there are still those *Pituophis* sold today that have been wild-caught, and most of these still do fairly well in captivity, but a small percentage of them never fully accept captive living and will fare very poorly. These are usually adult specimens that have spent so much time in nature that their habits simply cannot be broken, and the animals themselves seem like they'd rather just whither away than learn to accept their new situation.

SOCIETIES

For the intermediate enthusiast, there are an array of organizations geared toward the keeping of reptiles and amphibians, virtually all of which will contain members who are familiar with the Pine Snakes and their kin. It is always nice to know others who share the same interests as you; if you meet people who live far enough away, you can learn a great deal about the *Pituophis* that are alien to your own locale. Such societies advertise in herpetological/herpetocultural magazines and journals, and are categorized variably, so there's a society for just about everyone—scientific groups (who work heavily on things like taxonomy, morphology, and genetics), keeping groups (who gear their energies towards the advancement of husbandry techniques), and natural history (simply learning about the animals themselves and how they live). You not only have to be part of a herp society, but can make valuable contributions as well. A lot of the information you may have about your animals, information that you may regard as no big deal, may turn out to be greatly valued by another society member. Don't keep such information all to yourself; share it! You can write for a newsletter or take photographs, or just read the newsletters and improve your own knowledge. Either way, there is a multitude of benefits to be reaped when joining a society, so don't avoid them.

SUGGESTED READING

RE-110

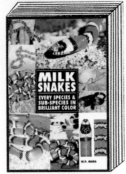

RE-107

RE-109

RE-124

RE-103

RE-108

RE-101

RE-106

RE-111

RE-112

RE-113

RE-104

RE-102

RE-131

RE-128

RE-136

TFH's fabulous "RE" series focuses in on the most fascinating reptiles and amphibians in the world. "RE" books are colorful, well-written, and very affordable. These and many other fine reptile and amphibian books can be found at your local pet shop.

...From T.F.H., the world's largest publisher of bird books, a new bird magazine for birdkeepers all over the world...

CAGED BIRD HOBBYIST
IS FOR EVERYONE
WHO LOVES BIRDS.

CAGED BIRD HOBBYIST
IS PACKED WITH VALUABLE
INFORMATION SHOWING HOW
TO FEED, HOUSE, TRAIN AND CARE
FOR ALL TYPES OF BIRDS.

Subscribe right now so you don't miss a single copy!

SM-316

INDEX

Page numbers in **boldface** refer to illustrations.